HOW DO ANiMALS USE... THEiR EARS?

Lynn Stone

Rourke
Publishing LLC
Vero Beach, Florida 32964

www.rourkepublishing.com

PHOTO CREDITS: All Photos © Lynn Stone

Editor: Robert Stengard-Olliges

Cover design by: Nicola Stratford, bdpublishing.com

Library of Congress Cataloging-in-Publication Data

Stone, Lynn M.
 How do animals use their ears? / Lynn Stone.
    p. cm. -- (How do animals use?)
 ISBN 978-1-60044-503-3
 1. Ear--Juvenile literature. 2. Animals--Juvenile literature. I. Title.
 QL948.S76 2008
 591.4'4--dc22
                                    2007016299

Printed in the USA

CG/CG

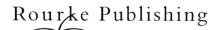

Rourke Publishing

www.rourkepublishing.com – rourke@rourkepublishing.com
Post Office Box 3328, Vero Beach, FL 32964

Animals hear with their ears.

Dog's ears listen for you to call them.

Deer's ears listen for danger.

Rabbit's ears listen
for predators.

Owl's ears listen for prey.

Elephants listen with big ear flaps.

13

Bears listen with little, furry ears.

14

Bullfrogs listen with big, round, flat ears.

Rabbits listen with long
floppy ears.

And some animal's ears tell us we better watch out.

21

Glossary

bear (bair) – a large animal with fur, sharp claws and teeth

bullfrog (BUL frawg) – a big frog that lives around water

deer (dir) – a brown mammal that can run very fast

dog (dawg) – an animial with four legs, a tail, and fur

elephant (EL uh fuhnt) – a very large mammal with a long nose called a trunk

owl (oul) – a bird with a large, round head

Index

Further Reading

Nunn, Daniel. *Ears*. Heinemann, 2007.
Perkins, Wendy. *Let's Look at Animal Ears*. Pebble
  Press, 2007.

Websites

www.kidsites.com/sites-edu/animals.htm
animal.discovery.com

About the Author

Lynn M. Stone is the author of more than 400 children's books. He is a talented natural history photographer as well. Lynn, a former teacher, travels worldwide to photograph wildlife in its natural habitat.